jams & jellies

IN LESS THAN 30 MINUTES

jams & jellies

IN LESS THAN 30 MINUTES

PAMELA BENNETT

GIBBS SMITH

TO ENRICH AND INSPIRE HUMANKIND

To my Mama, Georgia Draughon Bennett, who could do anything
and inspired her children to feel they could do the same.

First Edition
15 14 13 12 11   5 4 3 2 1

Text © 2011 Pamela Bennett
Photographs © 2011 Joyce Oudkerk Pool

Published by
Gibbs Smith
P.O. Box 667
Layton, Utah 84041

1.800.835.4993 orders
www.gibbs-smith.com

Cover and Book Design by Michelle Farinella Design
Printed and bound in China

Gibbs Smith books are printed on either recycled, 100% post-consumer waste, FSC-certified papers or on paper produced from sustainable PEFC-certified forest/controlled wood source. Learn more at www.pefc.org.

Library of Congress Cataloging-in-Publication Data

Bennett, Pamela.
  Jams & jellies in less than 30 minutes / Pamela Bennett ; photographs, Joyce Oudkerk Pool. — 1st ed.
     p. cm.
  Includes index.
  ISBN 978-1-4236-1871-3
  1. Jam. 2. Jelly. I. Title. II. Title: Jams and jellies in less than thirty minutes.
  TX612.J3B45 2011
  641.8'52—dc22

                              2010030689

The author and publisher assume no legal or moral responsibility for the outcome or performance of these recipes in your home kitchen, or for the quality or safety of the end product. Many factors present in a home kitchen situation, from the quality and freshness of the fruit to the cleanliness of the utensils and preparation space, can affect the safety of the product.

CONTENTS

Introduction

For the cook who loves to serve something deliciously homemade but has little time to spare, *Jams and Jellies in Less Than 30 Minutes* is the answer—for parties, for holiday meals, and for every day. You'll have the satisfaction that comes from serving homemade jam and jelly without the fuss of canning. People will think you spent hours on a difficult chore when it really wasn't hard at all.

Whether you're new to the kitchen or a veteran cook, you will take genuine delight in creating these small-batch jams and jellies that are not only mouthwatering but beautiful as well. In less than a half hour and in very few steps, you can mix up a sweet treat to savor or to share. A pretty dish of your new kitchen creation can dress up a dinner table. Unused portions can be safely refrigerated for three to four weeks.

Here are methods and recipes for 55 delectable sweet treats that will garner compliments from dinner guests and praise from the family at snack time or mealtime. A small jar of specially made jelly will endear you to any hostess who receives it as a gift, and the delicious, sweet aftertaste of your concoctions will put your name admiringly on the tongues of all your friends who like to talk about food.

These recipes offer creative possibilities as limitless as your imagination. The jams are as delicious in the morning on bagels or croissants as they are served during an elegant brunch or bridal shower. And in many cases they can complement the perfect roast or grilled meat, turn a marinade or sauce from plain to extraordinary, or make an amazing topping for a dish of ice cream.

Tasters have declared that some of these recipes are as decadent as a bowl of chocolate truffles, while others have affirmed the fruity spreads to be as delicious as any delectable candy they've ever sampled. If your experience with jams and jellies has been limited to basic grape or strawberry, then your jam/jelly world has thus far been colored in terms of gray. When you cook from this book, be prepared for a rainbow of taste explosions! Whether your preference is sweet or savory, familiar or exotic, this collection was made for you. The ingredients you'll need are readily available, and each recipe can be simply prepared without intimidation.

Once you get organized, you can make jam or jelly in less than 30 minutes from start to finish! Make one in the morning and serve it that evening to your family, or wow guests at a dinner party or brunch or holiday festivity . . . the possibilities are endless. With these instructions and recipes as your guide, you're on your way to creating your own memorable signature jams and jellies. You'll be amazed at these "little masterpieces in a jar."

A BASIC LESSON IN JAMS & JELLIES

Jams and jellies are made from fruits, preserved by sugar, and jelled (thickened). To achieve proper jelling, you must find the right balance of four components: fruit, acid, sugar, and pectin. *Pectin* is made from apples. It causes the jell to form. All fruits contain some pectin—apples, grapes, and plums contain enough *natural* pectin to form a jell (sometimes called a "set") on their own. However, other fruits, like cherries, blackberries, and strawberries, contain very little natural pectin, so they need the addition of pectin that you purchase.

Plain granulated sugar is the sweetener most used in jams and jellies. It is important that you do *not* reduce the amount of sugar in any of these recipes. You might think that by doing so you will save on caloric intake, or perhaps you think the recipe requires "too much sugar" for your family. However, a deviation from the amount of sugar called for in the recipe can cause runny jam. Even more important, sugar acts as a preservative; if the correct amount of sugar is not used, yeasts and molds can develop and cause spoilage.

An acid component is also critical to jell formation. With too little acid, your jell will never set. Too much acid can cause the jell to "weep," or liquid to separate from the jam around the edges. Lemon juice is the predominant acid used in jelling. Some recipes may call for lime juice, or occasionally vinegar can be used.

Most recipes in this book call for pectin as the jelling agent, although some call for gelatin. I offer some simple guidelines regarding pectin:

Pectin is available in liquid and powder form, 3½-ounce size. Liquid and powdered pectin work equally well but produce slightly different textures of jam. This book suggests liquid and powder for different recipes; my personal preference is for the powdered form. Generally, liquid pectin works better in "clear" jellies, while powdered pectin works well with jam/jelly that has several fruits. Pectin can be found in the canning supplies section of most grocery stores. While all brands will do the job of thickening your product, they produce slightly different textures. Experiment with different brands to see which you like best.

Pectin has a limited shelf life and packages are stamped with an expiration date. Old pectin might not result in a jell because it loses its potency over time.

Jams and jellies continue to set for up to 24 hours after you've poured them into the jars. So don't fret if it seems too runny at the time of pouring.

JAR PREPARATION

Follow these easy steps to ensure the jars are sterile:

- Place all newly purchased jam/jelly jars in the top rack of your dishwasher. Also include the two-piece lids with bands. Wash on one complete cycle, including a hot cycle. This will sterilize the jars. (Alternatively, you can wash jars in hot soapy water and then pour in boiling water to sterilize them. Be careful not to burn yourself when pouring out the hot water. Drain upside down.)

- Allow jars to cool, and handle as little as possible, thus allowing them to remain sterile. Kitchen tongs prove helpful but are not required.

- When making cooked jams, place the empty jar(s) on a cookie sheet or mat to protect your countertop. Remember to always leave at least $\frac{1}{4}$ inch headspace when filling jars to allow for expansion of the jelly when it gets cold.

- Screw the two-piece lids and bands onto your jars to keep the product fresh and clean until ready to serve.

Jams and jellies made from recipes in this book must be stored in your refrigerator or freezer (the individual recipe will so indicate). They are *not* to be stored without proper refrigeration. Because these products are not sealed in their jars through a heat process, they need to be consumed within the time period noted at the bottom of each recipe. Beyond this period, they should not be considered safe for consumption.

Helpful Hint: always make jelly on a clear day rather than a cloudy or stormy day. Weather affects the appearance.

Berry Jams

Blueberry Spice Jam

Pancakes or waffles await your generous pouring.

Yield 6 (½ pint) jars

4½ cups blueberries
Juice of 1 lemon
¼ teaspoon cinnamon

1 tablespoon freshly grated gingerroot
7 cups sugar
1 pouch liquid pectin

Wash blueberries and crush them. Place in a large saucepan.

Add lemon juice, cinnamon and gingerroot.

Add sugar.

Mix thoroughly and heat rapidly to a full boil.

Continue to boil for approximately 2 minutes, stirring constantly.

Remove from stove and add pectin. Stir.

Skim foam from the top.

Pour into jars and cover tightly.

Refrigerate for up to 3–4 weeks.

Lemon Blueberry Jam

Absolutely divine with lemon muffins, bagels, or French toast.

Yield 6 (½ pint) jars

4½ cups blueberries
  (may use fresh or frozen)
7 cups sugar

Juice and zest of 1 large lemon
3 pouches liquid pectin

If berries are fresh, rinse and place in saucepan. If berries are frozen, don't rinse or thaw. Crush slightly.

Stir in sugar, lemon juice, and zest.

Bring to a boil on medium-high, stirring constantly. Continue a full boil for approximately 1 minute.

Stir in pectin and return to a full boil for 1 minute more.

Pour into sterilized jars and cover tightly with lids. Cool before refrigerating.

Keeps for up to 4 weeks in refrigerator.

Your window of opportunity for fresh blueberries is generally brief (June through August), so if you're a lover of this delicious, rich-in-antioxidant fruit, buy several pints and follow these directions to _freeze_, for a decadent jam you can make in snowy February:

Rinse blueberries and carefully pat dry.

Allow to "air" dry for 5–10 minutes.

Place the berries on a clean dish towel on a cookie sheet; don't crowd them, or they'll freeze stuck together.

Freeze for 4–5 hours.

Transfer the frozen berries to a zipper lock bag or a jar with a twist-off top.

Freeze for up to one year (if you can resist that long!).

Blackberry Jam

Lucky enough to pick your own blackberries? This jam is worth enduring prickly thorns, a hot sun, and red bugs lying in wait to keep you up itching all night. This blackberry treat is succulent on biscuits, ice cream, and hoecakes. Yummmmm.

Yield 4 (½ pint) jars

3 cups fresh blackberries
1 package powdered pectin
4 ½ cups sugar
2 tablespoons lemon juice

Crush the blackberries with a fork or potato masher (do *not* use a food processor) and place in a heavy saucepan.

Add the pectin and begin stirring constantly on high heat until mixture is boiling throughout, not just around the edge of the pan.

Add the sugar and lemon juice, and return to boiling. Boil at least 1 full minute, stirring constantly.

Remove from heat and skim the foam from the top.

Spoon into prepared sterilized jars and cover tightly.

When jars have cooled, store in refrigerator for up to 4 weeks.

Winter Triple Berry

Thanks to frozen berries, you can make this hearty jam anytime of the year. It's yummy with breads and delicious as a dip for sliced fruit.

Yield 6–7 cups

1 package (12 ounces) frozen raspberries

1 package (12 ounces) frozen blackberries

1 package (12 ounces) frozen strawberries

Or:

2 large packages (32–36 ounces total) combined/mixed frozen berries

Juice of 1 small lemon

4 cups sugar, divided

1 package powdered pectin

Thaw the frozen berries in separate bowls, keeping the juice with the berries.

Crush the berries in their juice, one bag at a time, in a large saucepan.

Add the lemon juice and stir.

Add half of the sugar and bring to full boil. Stir constantly for 5 minutes.

Add remaining sugar and stir. Bring back to a boil.

Add the pectin and continue boiling, stirring constantly, 1 minute. Remove from heat and skim foam from the top.

Pour into sterilized jars.

Will keep in refrigerator for up to 3 weeks.

Framboise Raspberry Jam

Makes a remarkable dessert topping. Also elegant on chewy rustic bread and delicious on French toast. To create a marinade for chicken, add 3 tablespoons red wine vinegar and 2 tablespoons canola oil to 1 cup jam.

Yield 4 (¹⁄₂ pint) jars

4¹⁄₂ cups fresh raspberries
3 cups sugar
¹⁄₄ cup Framboise (raspberry brandy)

Place all ingredients in a heavy saucepan over medium heat.

Bring to a boil, stirring occasionally.

When the mixture boils, raise heat to high, stirring constantly for 20 minutes. Don't let this stick!

When jam-like consistency has been achieved, immediately remove from heat. (Jam will thicken as it cools.)

Pour into hot, sterilized jars and cover tightly.

Can be refrigerated up to 6 weeks, thanks to fermentation. But don't count on it lasting that long!

NOTE: YOU CAN SUBSTITUTE PEACHES OR NECTARINES FOR PART OF THE RASPBERRIES, IF YOU LIKE.

No-Cook Strawberry Jam

Never met a biscuit it didn't like. For a delicious salad vinaigrette, combine ½ cup jam with 1 tablespoon red wine vinegar and 3 tablespoons olive oil.

Yield 1½ pints

2 cups mashed strawberries
2 cups sugar
1 package powdered pectin
2 tablespoons lemon juice
3–4 drops red food coloring

To the berries, add sugar. Stir to coat berries well. Let stand for 10 minutes, stirring occasionally, while the berries release their juice.

Add the pectin, lemon juice, and food coloring. Mix well and stir constantly for 3 minutes.

Spoon jam into jars or plastic containers. Cover tightly.

Will keep for 1 year in the freezer or 3 weeks in the refrigerator.

NOTE: OTHER BERRIES CAN BE SUBSTITUTED, SUCH AS RASPBERRIES OR BLACKBERRIES, IN THE SAME AMOUNT.

Flowers & Strawberry Jam

Perfect for a picnic basket. Make it that morning and take along to a neighborhood cookout or potluck gathering. Folks will not believe you made this; yet it's simple and deliciously eye appealing.

Yield 1 pint

1 pound strawberries, slightly under ripe

3 cups sugar

Juice of 4 small lemons

½ cup edible flowers (such as rose petals, nasturtiums, violets, four o'clocks)*

1 pouch liquid pectin

Bring the strawberries, sugar, and lemon juice to a boil, stirring constantly until sugar is dissolved.

Add the edible flower petals and boil for 2 minutes.

Add the pectin and stir constantly for 1 minute more.

Fill sterilized jars and place several uncooked beautiful petals or blossoms on top of the jam before covering tightly.

Refrigerate for up to 3 weeks.

*Edible flowers are available at natural food stores, or you can select from your own garden. The website *ask.com* will steer you away from any poisonous or dangerous blossoms.

Fruit Preserves

Freezer Black Cherry Jam

Waffles and pancakes are made for this jam. Pan-fried pork chops get a boost when covered with jam for the final minutes of cooking, creating a wonderful glaze.

Yield 1 quart freezer container

3 cups black cherries, pitted and coarsely chopped
5 cups sugar
1 package powdered pectin
1 cup water

In a large bowl, mix cherries and sugar together. Let stand 20 minutes while cherries release their juice.

In a small saucepan, combine pectin and water. Boil for 1 minute, stirring constantly.

Add pectin to cherries and stir for 2 minutes.

Pour into freezer containers.

Keeps for up to 4 months in the freezer.

Cranberry-Pear Relish

Perfect accompaniment for cranberry bread during fall celebrations such as a Halloween breakfast or Thanksgiving dinner. Also great as a side dish with baked squash, creamy green beans, and cheesy potatoes.

Yield 2 (¹⁄₂ pint) jars

8 ounces (about 3 cups) fresh cranberries
2 small firm pears
1 tablespoon honey
¹⁄₂ cup sugar
¹⁄₂ small lemon, quartered
Dash salt

Wash cranberries.

Peel and core pears.

In a food processor, chop cranberries and pears with honey, sugar, lemon, and salt.

Transfer to a smaller container, cover tightly, and chill.

Keeps in refrigerator for 1–2 weeks.

Just Peachy

Biscuits, oh my! And it tastes even better over homemade churned vanilla ice cream!

Yield 4 (½ pint) jars

2½–3 pounds fresh peaches
1½ cups sugar
3 teaspoons lemon juice

Wash and peel the peaches; remove pits.

Cut into slices or chop, your preference.

Cover peaches with all of the sugar and let stand for 10 minutes while fruit releases its juice.

In a medium saucepan, combine peach mixture and lemon juice. Cook over moderately high heat for 20-plus minutes. Stir continuously so it doesn't stick.

When appearance is syrupy, pour into clean hot jars and cover tightly. Let cool before refrigerating.

Keeps in refrigerator for 3–4 weeks.

Pear-Apple Jam

"Sweetly and subtly perfumed a delicacy." England's King Henry II's desire for pears obliged that they be shipped to his castle from a thousand miles away. Try this mouthwatering jam and you'll understand why pears are a royal delight. Also makes a good marinade for a less-than expensive roast.

Yield 3 (½ pint) jars

2 cups pears
1 cup apples, peeled
¼ teaspoon cinnamon

6 ½ cups sugar
⅓ cup lemon juice
2 pouches liquid pectin

Finely chop the pears and apples. Crush them in a large saucepan.

Stir cinnamon into the fruit.

Mix sugar and lemon juice into the fruit mixture and bring to a boil, stirring constantly.

Add pectin immediately and return to a boil for 1 full minute, stirring constantly.

Remove from heat and skim foam.

Pour into sterilized jars and cover tightly.

Refrigerate for up to 3 weeks.

Ginger Pear Jam

Like a good marriage, pear and ginger are two lovebirds that can stand very well on their own; but when paired together, what a union! Breakfast never had it so good.

Yield 4 (½ pint) jars

2 pounds pears, cores removed

½ cup chopped candied ginger bits

5 ⅓ cups sugar

1 ¼ cups water

Juice of 2 small lemons

1 teaspoon freshly grated gingerroot

Dice the pears and place into a large saucepan.

Add candied ginger, sugar, and water.

Cook on medium heat until sugar has dissolved. Increase heat and bring to a rapid boil for about 10 minutes, stirring occasionally.

Add the lemon juice and freshly grated ginger.

Fill sterilized jars and cool before refrigerating.

Keeps in refrigerator for up to 3 weeks.

Plum Crazy

With or without the optional chipotle peppers, this jam is divine on biscuits. Mix with softened cream cheese, shape into a ball, and roll in chopped nuts of your choice (pecans, walnuts, almonds) for a great appetizer to serve with assorted fresh vegetables and crackers.

Yield 3 pints

2 pounds fresh plums
1 tablespoon lemon juice
1 pouch liquid pectin

½ cup water
5 cups sugar
1 small chipotle pepper, diced (*optional*)

Wash plums, remove pits, and chop. Place in a large saucepan.

Mix in lemon juice and pectin. Cook over medium heat while the plums liquefy, about 10 minutes.

Add the water, increase heat, and continue to cook until boiling.

Skim foam from the top.

Add the sugar and boil for 10–15 minutes more, until it reaches a syrup-like consistency.

Add the chipotle peppers, if desired.

Pour into hot sterilized bottles.

Let cool completely. Refrigerate.

Keeps for 3–4 weeks in refrigerator.

Rhubarb-Strawberry Jam

Slabs of thick bread or pancakes made on a late Saturday morning will make you glad you went to the farmers market for those stalks of rhubarb.

Yield 2½ pints

3 cups rhubarb
3 cups strawberries
6 cups sugar, divided

1 tablespoon lemon juice
1 package powdered pectin

Scrub, wash, and chop the rhubarb. Place in a large saucepan.

Wash the strawberries and remove their caps.

Mash the berries with a fork or potato masher and add to the rhubarb.

Add 4 cups of sugar and the lemon juice and mix well.

Cook on medium-high heat, stirring occasionally, until boiling, approximately 4–5 minutes.

Stir in remaining sugar and pectin. Boil for 5 minutes* longer, stirring frequently.

Pour into hot, prepared jars and cover tightly with two-piece lids.

Allow to cool, then refrigerate. Will keep in refrigerator for 2–3 weeks.

*The longer you cook this mixture, the thicker it becomes. Stop the cooking when the jam is a consistency you like. And remember, it will get thicker as it cools.

Cranberry Jam

Thanksgiving leftovers are better with this as a side. It's extra good on plain white cakes, hoecakes, and corn bread.

Yield 3 pints

2 pounds fresh cranberries

2 large Red or Golden Delicious
  apples*

4 cups sugar

2 cups water

Juice and zest of 1 small lemon

Wash cranberries and discard any bruised berries.

Chop apples and add to cranberries in a large cooking pot with sugar and water.

Boil for 10–15 minutes.

Skim the foam from the top and discard.

Add the lemon juice and zest to the mixture.

Simmer until thickened, 5 or more minutes, stirring often.

Place in jars, cover tightly, and let cool.

Can be refrigerated for 3–4 weeks.

*Use a "soft" apple such as the *Delicious* varieties; hard apples do not work as well.

NOTE: PECTIN IS NOT NEEDED SINCE BOTH CRANBERRIES AND APPLES CONTAIN ADEQUATE AMOUNTS OF NATURAL PECTIN.

Red Cherry Jam

Dresses up English muffins and toast. Also makes a scrumptious glaze for baked ham: just pour the jam all over the meat and let the oven do the hard work.

Yield 3 pints

4 cups chopped red cherries	½ teaspoon cinnamon
1 package powdered pectin	½ teaspoon ground cloves
¼ cup lemon juice	4 ½ cups sugar
1 teaspoon salt	

Wash cherries, discard stems, and remove pits. Chop into small bits.

Put all ingredients except the sugar into a large kettle. Bring to a full rolling boil that can't be stirred down.

Immediately add sugar. Bring mixture to a full rolling boil and cook for 2 more minutes, stirring constantly.

Skim the foam from the top.

Pour into hot sterilized jars and cover tightly. Let cool.

Refrigerate for up to 3 weeks.

Fig Jam

Such a beautiful ending to a meal: serve with an assortment of great cheeses, a variety of crackers, and select pieces of fruit.

Yield 6 (½ pint) jars

5 pounds (about two quarts) chopped fresh figs
6 cups sugar
¾ cup water
¼ cup lemon juice

Cover chopped figs with boiling water. Cool enough to peel skins and discard.

Chop figs. Let stand 10 minutes, then drain. If figs are still too coarse, process in a blender.

In a large pot, combine figs, sugar, and water. Slowly bring to a boil on medium heat, stirring until the sugar dissolves.

Raise heat to medium-high and cook rapidly until thickened, stirring constantly to prevent sticking.

Add lemon juice and cook 1 minute.

Pour in hot sterilized jars. Cover tightly.

Cool completely before refrigerating.

Keeps 3–4 weeks in refrigerator.

Cantaloupe Jam

Cantaloupe Jam

When the season provides us with the bounty of luscious melons, this jam is a treat. Flavors burst when served on warm nut breads, lemon muffins, or English muffins.

Yield 4 cups

2 medium cantaloupes (very soft but not overripe)
1½ cups sugar
Juice and zest of 1 small lemon
Dash salt

Scoop the softened cantaloupe into a blender and pulse just a few seconds until it reaches the consistency of thick cake batter. Do not over blend or the cantaloupe will become too runny.

Put this mixture into a heavy saucepan and blend in all other ingredients. Cook for 30 minutes on medium heat, stirring continuously.

Pour into sterilized jars and cover tightly.

Keeps in the refrigerator for up to 3 weeks.

NOTE: THE LONGER YOU STIR THIS MIXTURE, THE THICKER IT WILL BECOME. THE DESIRED CONSISTENCY IS SOMEWHERE BETWEEN A COTTAGE CHEESE CURD AND A SPREADABLE BUTTER OR SOFT JAM.

No-Cook Peachy Orange Jam

This summer treat is so easy and requires so little of your time in the kitchen, you almost feel guilty for accepting kudos for the luscious concoction. So enjoy your time saved and relax by the pool.

Yield 3–4 (½ pint) jars

1 large orange, grated and zest
   reserved

2½ cups finely chopped peaches

⅓ cup maraschino cherries,
   halved or quartered

2 tablespoons lemon juice

5 cups sugar

¾ cup water

1 package powdered pectin

Section the orange and remove the pithy parts. Dice the sections and place in a bowl along with the zest.

Add the peaches, cherries, lemon juice, and sugar, and mix well. Let stand for 10 minutes while the fruits release their liquid.

In a small saucepan, combine water with pectin. Boil for 1 minute.

Stir pectin into the fruit mixture for 3 minutes, or until the sugar is dissolved.

Pour into sterilized jars and cover tightly. Let stand at room temperature until set (depending on altitude, this could take up to 24 hours). Then refrigerate.

Keeps in refrigerator for up to 3 weeks.

Pear-Cranberry Jam

The aroma of this jam evokes memories of jumping in raked leaves, the first autumn fire in the chimney, and yummy snacks after winning that overtime football game in the backyard. Make some of your own autumn memories with this rich jam.

Yield 2–3 (½ pint) jars

1½ cups cranberries, fresh or frozen
4 pears
5 cups sugar

½ cup water
1 package powdered pectin
¼ cup sherry *(optional)*

Place cranberries in a food processor and pulse until they are coarsely chopped. Transfer to a large saucepan.

Peel and finely chop the pears (hand chop only; a processor turns pears to mush). Add to the cranberries.

Stir sugar into the fruit and let stand for 10 minutes.

Combine water, pectin, and sherry (optional) in a separate saucepan. Bring to a boil and cook for 1 minute, stirring constantly.

Stir pectin into the fruit mixture. Bring to a boil and cook for 3 minutes, stirring constantly.

Pour jam into sterilized jars and cover tightly.

Let stand at room temperature until the jam sets, up to 24 hours.

Keeps up to 3 weeks in the refrigerator and several months in the freezer.

Apricot Jam

Does any color in the spectrum rival the bold, rich apricot? It says, "Look at me! I'm as beautiful as the setting sun." This jam is what an apricot is born to become.

Yield 2 (½ pint) jars

2 cups dried apricot halves
2½ cups water
Juice and zest of 1 large orange

1¼ cups sugar
1 teaspoon almond extract
3 tablespoons brandy or cognac
(optional)

Combine apricots and water in a bowl. Cover and let stand overnight.

Place apricots and their soaking water into a saucepan with orange juice and zest. Simmer for about 5 minutes.

Add the sugar and bring to a boil. Stir often until mixture is thick. Don't allow the mixture to cook to a puree! Bits of apricot should be visible.

Remove from heat after approximately 25 minutes, and add the almond extract and brandy, if using.

Pour into sterilized jars and cover tightly.

Keeps in refrigerator for up to 4 weeks.

Mock Raspberry Jam aka Green Tomato Jelly

This is a star! Southern depression-era cooks longed for the taste of raspberries, but such delicacies were scarce. So they improvised, using what their country gardens had in abundance—green tomatoes! Dozens have tasted my version and no one has ever guessed that no raspberries were harmed in its creation!

Yield 4–6 (½ pint) jars

5 cups finely chopped green tomatoes
4 cups sugar
6 ounces (2 small packages) raspberry Jell-O

Measure tomatoes into a large saucepan.

Add sugar and bring to a boil over medium heat; let cook for 15 minutes, stirring frequently.

Skim foam from the top and discard.

Add the Jell-O and stir well so the mixture doesn't stick to the pan. Bring to a low boil and boil for 1 minute.

Pour into sterilized jars and cover tightly. Let cool before refrigerating.

Keeps in refrigerator for about 3 weeks.

Crocodile Tears

Have a child who's a picky eater? They'll be mesmerized by your tall tale of the pirate and the crocodile—Peter Pan's or your own version. Serve with a platter of fresh fruit, cheeses, and crackers. Children love the grape "eyes" and coconut "tears."

Yield 2 (½ pint) jars

1 small Granny Smith apple

2 cups sweetened apple juice

2 tablespoons lime juice

½ cup sugar

½ cup green grapes

¾ cup flaked coconut

1 teaspoon red pepper flakes

3 drops yellow food coloring

1 drop green food coloring

Core and dice the apple. Place apple, apple juice, and lime juice in a medium saucepan. Cook over medium-high heat for about 10 minutes while the apple softens.

Add the sugar and cook until dissolved and there is no evidence of sugar granules.

Add the grapes, coconut, pepper flakes, and food coloring. Stir and cook for 15–20 minutes while it jells.

Pour into sterilized jars, seal tightly, and let cool.

Refrigerate for up to 1 week.

Citrus & Tropical Jellies & Jams

Pineapple Pleasure

This is good with *nan* (Indian bread), and flatbreads, or with grilled veggies stuffed in a pita pocket. It's also wonderful poured generously over a ham before baking or over fish before grilling.

Yield 2 (½ pint) jars

1 can (20 ounces) crushed pineapple, with juice
2 cups sugar
1 teaspoon cinnamon

Pour all ingredients together into a heavy saucepan and cook for 20–30 minutes, stirring constantly. Be careful not to let it stick to the pan.

Pour into prepared sterilized jars. Let cool, then refrigerate.

Will keep for 2 weeks in refrigerator.

Southern Ambrosia Jam

Pure decadence on croissants or muffins at brunch. You'll receive rave reviews when used as a topping for pound cake or angel food cake. My Texan husband swears it's the best vanilla ice-cream topping on the planet. Delicious with all holiday meals!

Yield 4–5 (½ pint) jars

1 can (32 ounces) crushed
    pineapple, drained
1 bag (7 ounces) shredded coconut
3 small oranges, peeled and
    chopped

1 small jar maraschino cherries
3 cups sugar
1½ cups water
1 package powdered pectin

In a large saucepan, mix together all ingredients except pectin.

Cook over medium-high heat, stirring frequently, for 10 minutes. Bring to a boil but not a hard, high boil.

Add pectin and boil for approximately 1 minute more.

Skim foam from top.

Pour into jars and refrigerate.

Keeps about 2 weeks refrigerated.

Orange or Lemon Jelly

Perfection on poppy seed or lemon muffins! I once used this jelly as an emergency marinade for grilling fish and it's now my go-to.

Yield 2–3 (½ pint) jars

2½ cups* orange juice
  or lemon juice
Zest from all the oranges or lemons

6 cups sugar
1 pouch liquid pectin

Combine juice and zest in a bowl and let stand for 10 minutes.

Pour juice into a large saucepan and add sugar. Mix thoroughly.

Heat rapidly to boiling. Add pectin at once and stir constantly.

Return to full rolling boil for ½ minute.

Remove from stove and skim off foam.

Pout into prepared jars and cover tightly. Let cool, then refrigerate.

Keeps in refrigerator for up to 3 weeks.

*Generally speaking, a medium orange or large lemon will produce about ¼ cup juice. You can substitute frozen orange juice or lemonade, but do not dilute with water.

Sour Orange Marmalade

Bagels beg for this! Also exquisite as a sauce for white fish or pork. To make a quick Asian salad dressing, add a splash of soy sauce and ½ teaspoon freshly grated ginger to ⅓–½ cup marmalade.

Yield 4 cups

6 medium-size sour oranges*	3 cups sugar
2 quarts water, plus	½ teaspoon salt

Remove peel from 2 oranges. Slice peel very thinly, place in a small saucepan, and cover with water. Boil until tender. Change the water often if the flavor becomes too bitter. Drain.

Peel remaining oranges. Boil pulp in 2 quarts of water until very soft. Strain.

In a large saucepan, mix juice with drained peel, sugar, and salt.

Bring to a boil. As mixtures boils, it will reach the jelly stage** in about 10 minutes.

Let stand until slightly cool.

Pour into sterilized jars and refrigerate immediately.

Will keep for up to 3 weeks.

*Sometimes Asian specialty grocers get a shipment of sour oranges, but generic under-ripe oranges work just as well. Shop for the orange whose taste hasn't yet developed its complete sweetness.

**There are three reliable ways to test for the jelly stage:

1. Insert your kitchen thermometer into the jam while cooking. The thermometer should read between 200 and 220 degrees F. When it does, you can carefully pour the jam into jars.

2. Jam/jelly is ready when a syrupy stage has been reached, generally after the final 1 minute of boiling. If the desired consistency hasn't been achieved, continue boiling beyond what the recipe says, until you notice a change in appearance, i.e., the jam is getting visibly thicker. Remember, the mixture will set as it cools.

3. The "cold plate" method is where you chill a plate in your freezer, remove it and dribble a few drops of prepared jam/jelly onto the plate. Return it to the freezer for 30 seconds to 1 minute. Remove the plate from the freezer. When you touch the drops of jam, the *surface* of the jam/jelly will feel like store-purchased jam/jelly, while *closer to the plate*, it will feel syrupy to the touch.

Papaya Tropics Jam

This is just wonderful when grilling fish (mahi mahi, tilapia), shrimp, or scallops, or brushed over pepper, onion, and pineapple slices. You'll be gilding the lily when you spread it onto warm banana bread.

Yield 2 (½ pint) jars

3 cups diced papaya*

1 banana, peeled

1½ cups sugar

¼ cup orange juice

1 package powdered pectin

Wash and peel the papayas. Discard seeds. Dice papayas and place in a large, heavy saucepan.

Mash the banana, leaving either small or large chunks, depending on your preference. Add to the papayas.

Stir in sugar and orange juice. Cook on medium-high, stirring constantly, until the sugar dissolves, about 10 minutes.

When the mixture comes to a full boil, add the pectin and continue stirring for 1 minute.

Fill the prepared jars and cover tightly. Let cool.

Can be refrigerated for up to 2 weeks.

*If fresh papayas are unavailable, you can substitute canned, but drain and discard the juice.

Mango Madness Spread

When I served a ladies lunch with soufflé, salad, muffins, and Mango Madness, you'd have thought I had sprinkled "happy dust" all around the table!

Yield 3 cups

4 large mangoes (soft, ripe)

3 cups sugar

¼ cup lemon juice (1 small lemon)

1 teaspoon ginger powder

¼ cup chopped candied ginger

1 package powdered pectin

Wash and peel the mangoes. Chop into manageable chunks and place in a blender or food processor.

Puree to consistency of cake batter—not too runny, leaving some chunks of mango visible. Pour into a deep saucepan.

Stir in the sugar and lemon juice.

Cook on medium heat for 10 minutes, stirring constantly, until sugar has dissolved and is no longer grainy.

Add the ginger powder and candied ginger. Cook for 5 minutes.

Just as the mixture begins to boil, add pectin, return to boiling, and stir continuously for 1 minute.

Pour into prepared sterilized jars and cover tightly.

Cool, then refrigerate for up to 2 weeks.

Pineapple-Carrot Jam

This jam is pretty and yummy. Bagels and morning breads love to partner with it.

Yield 2 (½ pint) jars

1 can (20 ounces) crushed pineapple, with juice
½ cup sugar
2 cups grated carrots
2 tablespoons fresh grated ginger
1 tablespoon lemon zest

Bring all ingredients except lemon zest to a boil in a 2-quart saucepan.

Reduce heat and simmer for 25–30 minutes, stirring occasionally, until mixture is the consistency of applesauce.

Stir in lemon zest.

Pour into sterilized jars and cover tightly.

Cool and refrigerate.

Will last up to 1 month in the refrigerator.

Grapefruit Marmalade

Such a small change from oranges to grapefruit renders an entirely different experience. The impact is unexpected and fresh. Delicious on scones.

Yield 2 (½ pint) jars

2 large grapefruit
1 large lemon
2 cups water
4 cups sugar

Zest and then peel grapefruit and lemon; remove pith.

Chop fruit coarsely. Place fruit, zest, and water in a large saucepan.

Simmer for about 10 minutes. Remove from heat and let cool.

Return grapefruit to moderate heat and add the sugar. Bring to a boil, stirring until the sugar dissolves.

Skim foam. Pour into sterilized jars and cover tightly. Let cool.

Keeps refrigerated for up to 3 weeks.

Herb & Savory Spreads

Onion Jam

So versatile! This jam elevates *osso buco* to a new level. It is put to good use in any slow-cooked Italian recipe (red sauce and clam sauce). When used in grilling veggies or as a marinade for pork or beef roasts, the flavors pop and compliments pour in.

Yield 2 (½ pint) jars

2 pounds* Vidalia or white onions
2 tablespoons olive oil
1 teaspoon salt

½ teaspoon black pepper
¾ cup sugar
½ cup white wine vinegar

Peel onions and chop to size according to your preference.

Heat oil in a deep frying pan, then add onions, salt, and pepper. Saute until onions become translucent, about 15 minutes.

Add sugar and cook until the onions become caramelized, about 10 minutes.

Add vinegar last and simmer for 5 minutes, stirring frequently so onions don't stick to the pan.

Spoon into prepared sterilized jars. Let cool before refrigerating.

Consume within 7–10 days.

*Best made in small batches for quality control.

Garlic Galore

This is so good you'll cry! Smooth it on a hearty French loaf or drizzle it onto veggies for baking or broiling. Spoon into soups, broths, or stews for added depth.

Yield 1 pint

4 large garlic bulbs

Juice and zest of 1 small lemon

1 cup white vinegar, divided

2 tablespoons olive oil

2 cups sugar

1 pouch liquid pectin

Remove and discard the husk from the garlic bulbs.

In a blender or food processor, combine the garlic, lemon juice, $\frac{1}{2}$ cup vinegar, and olive oil. Process until smooth.

In a large saucepan, combine the garlic mixture with remaining vinegar, sugar, and lemon zest.

Bring this mixture to a boil and continue stirring.

Add the pectin and boil rapidly for 1 minute, stirring constantly.

Pour mixture into sterilized jars and cover tightly.

Can be refrigerated for up to 2 weeks.

Jalapeño Jelly

A huge helping of corn bread, a bowl of chili, your favorite ice-cold drink with bead drops running down the glass . . . ahhh . . . life is good. If there's any of this jelly left over, serve it with your Latin or Mexican dishes; it's fabulous mixed with cream cheese as a dip for tortilla chips.

Yield 2–3 (1/2 pint) jars

1 large green bell pepper
1/2 cup jalapeño pepper
5 cups sugar

1 1/2 cups apple cider vinegar
2 pouches liquid pectin
3 drops green food coloring*

Seed and mince both peppers. Discard seeds and ribs.

Place peppers in a large saucepan. Add sugar and vinegar, and bring to a boil, stirring occasionally.

Continue a full rolling boil for 3 minutes, stirring frequently.

Add the pectin and stir continuously for 2 minutes.

Allow mixture to cool for 2 minutes, then stir again for 1 full minute to distribute peppers throughout the jelly mixture.

Pour into sterilized jars and cover tightly with two-piece lids.

Keeps in refrigerator for 3 weeks.

* If bolder green color is desired, add 3 drops green food coloring.

Inferno Jelly

A pepper's heat is its badge of honor in my family's Southern and Texas roots. This jelly slathered on top of corn bread is what the phrase "match made in heaven" is all about.

Yield 1 pint

2 small fresh chipotle chiles
1 small habanero chile
2 small serrano chiles
¼ cup water
2½ cups sugar

¼ cup lime juice
1 pouch liquid or 1 package
   powered pectin
2 drops red food coloring *(optional)*

Chop all of the chiles and place in a heavy saucepan along with the water. Cook on medium heat, stirring constantly, for about 10 minutes.

Add the sugar and lime juice and continue stirring until the sugar has dissolved completely.

Add pectin and food coloring, if desired. Stir vigorously over high heat for 1 minute.

Skim the foam from the top and remove from heat.

Pour into sterilized jars, cover tightly, and allow to cool.

Keeps in refrigerator for up to 4 weeks.

NOTE: WEAR DISPOSABLE KITCHEN GLOVES WHEN PREPARING THE CHILIES. AVOID TOUCHING YOUR EYES AND MOUTH DURING THIS PREPARATION.

Lavender Jam

My daughter's thirst-quenching lavender lemonade inspired me to make this Lavender Jam. It's one of my favorites and is always a hit. The fragrance and appearance are so professional; you couldn't possibly have made this yourself, could you? So perfect on croissants, English muffins, or alongside that favorite gourmet cheese. Elegantly beautiful for a bridal luncheon, baby shower, or formal afternoon tea.

Yield 2 (½ pint) jars

1½ cups water, divided
Juice of 1 medium lemon
1 cup firmly packed lavender
    blossoms*

2½ cups sugar
1 package powdered pectin

In a blender, whirl ¾ cup water, lemon juice, and lavender blossoms until the mixture resembles a smooth paste.

Slowly add the sugar and blend until dissolved. Pour mixture into a small saucepan.

Stir in the pectin and ¾ cup water. Bring to a boil and cook for 1 minute.

Quickly pour into sterilized jars and cover tightly. Let cool.

Keeps refrigerated for up to 3 weeks or frozen for up to 1 year.

*Available year-round at herb shops. In season, you can substitute violet blossoms.

Beet Jelly

This unusually savory jelly is wonderful with holiday turkey or ham. If you're lucky, there will be some to use with leftovers, but don't count on it.

Yield 1 pint

1 can (14 ounces) beets (not pickled)
1 package (3 ounces) orange Jell-O
1 tablespoon sugar
½ cup boiling water
1 tablespoon horseradish

Drain beets and cut julienne-style. Place in a medium saucepan. Heat gently.

Stir Jell-O and sugar into water until Jell-O has dissolved. Add to beets.

Add horseradish and stir to blend.

Chill in a pretty mold for a few hours before turning out to serve.

Keeps refrigerated for up to 2 weeks.

Tomato-Ginger Jam

My kitchen helpers said this was the best bruschetta spread they'd ever sampled.

Yield 1 pint

2 cups crushed tomatoes
   (fresh or canned)
2 tablespoons lime juice
1 tablespoon red wine vinegar
1 cup sugar
2 tablespoons freshly grated
   gingerroot

1 tablespoon chopped fresh basil
1 clove garlic, minced
2 tablespoons red pepper flakes
   or hot sauce
1 package powdered pectin

Combine all ingredients except pectin and cook (do not boil) over medium-high heat for 15 minutes, stirring constantly.

Add pectin and stir for 1 minute more.

Remove from heat and cool. Pout into sterilized jars and cover tightly. Refrigerate.

Keeps for 1 week in refrigerator.

Pumpkin Jam

Especially good on zucchini or pumpkin bread. Try stirring a couple tablespoons of it into oatmeal with raisins, or use as a filling for little tarts.

Yield 3 (½ pint) jars

1 can (16 ounces) pumpkin
4–6 oranges, grated and zest
 reserved
3 cups sugar

4 tablespoons caramel topping
3 teaspoons lemon juice
2 teaspoons cinnamon
1 pouch liquid pectin

Scoop pumpkin into a medium-size pot.

Peel zested oranges and remove white pithy parts. Chop the oranges and add to the pot.

Add all other ingredients, then simmer for 10 minutes, stirring frequently.

Add the orange zest and stir gently to distribute throughout.

Pour into jars and cover tightly.

Keeps in refrigerator for up to 2 weeks.

Jellies from Juice & Wine

Cinnamon Apple Jelly

Recruit your children or grandchildren to help you make this simple jelly. Children especially like adding the food coloring, and they'll remember this kitchen experience long after the cleanup. Good stuff on home-baked bread or poured over warm baked apples.

Yield 1 pint

1 teaspoon unflavored gelatin

1 2/3 cups unsweetened apple juice, divided

2 teaspoons lemon juice

1 stick cinnamon

1 drop yellow food coloring

1 drop red food coloring

5 tablespoons plus 1 teaspoon sugar

Bloom, or soften, the gelatin in 1/4 cup apple juice.

Combine remaining apple juice, lemon juice, cinnamon stick and food coloring in a saucepan. Boil approximately 7–8 minutes to reduce by one-third. Remove from heat.

Stir in sugar and softened gelatin until they dissolve.

Discard cinnamon stick.

Pour into sterilized jars. Cover tightly.

Store in refrigerator for up to 3 weeks.

Grape Jelly

Who didn't fall in love with jam and jelly for the first time when your lips were smeared with rich, sweet grape jelly on a peanut butter sandwich? Well, it's time to make your own grape jelly and fall in love all over again. Concord grapes are one of the great harvests of early autumn. These luscious beauties usually are not found at grocery stores, but you might find them at farmers markets. If your search is futile, or if you want to make this jelly in, say, midwinter, you can use frozen Concord grape juice as your base.

Yield 4 pints

8 cups Concord grapes   3 tablespoons lemon juice
6 cups sugar

Wash grapes and mash with either a potato masher or food processor.

Place in a deep saucepan, adding the sugar and lemon juice.

Bring to a low boil and watch carefully for 25 minutes, stirring frequently.

Strain through a sieve, then pour into sterilized jars and cover tightly.

The longer this sets, the firmer it will become, so avoid moving the jars for several hours. The humidity of your region will affect how long it takes the jam to jell. Refrigerate when you're satisfied with the "set."

Keeps for up to 4 weeks in the refrigerator.

Mint Jelly

Just as good for "dainty" company sandwiches of cucumber/tomato/watercress, Black Forest ham, or Greek gyros as for basting that perfect lamb for grilling or roasting.

Yield 2 (¹⁄₂ pint) jars

¹⁄₂ cup tightly packed mint leaves

¹⁄₂ cup vinegar

1 cup water

3 drops green food coloring

3¹⁄₂ cups sugar

1 package powered pectin

In a medium saucepan, combine mint leaves, vinegar, water, and food coloring.

Add sugar, stir, and bring to a rolling boil over medium-high heat for 15 minutes, stirring constantly.

Add pectin and return to a boil for ¹⁄₂ minute, stirring constantly.

Strain mint leaves and pour jelly into sterilized jars. Cover tightly.

Keeps in the refrigerator for up to 1 month.

Lime Jelly

Sweet-tooth cravings satisfied! Muffins and pancakes look appetizing, and not just on St. Patrick's Day. Also delicious with crackers and cream cheese.

Yield 1 pint

3 cups sugar
1 cup water
6 ounces frozen limeade, thawed
2 tablespoons lemon juice

5 drops green food coloring
2 drops yellow food coloring
1 pouch liquid pectin

Stir sugar and water together in a large saucepan. Bring to a boil, stirring occasionally. Allow to boil for 1 extra minute, then remove from heat.

Stir in limeade, lemon juice, and food colorings.

Add pectin and boil for 1 minute, stirring. Skim foam from the top.

Pour jelly into sterilized jars and cover tightly.

Cool to room temperature.

Can be stored in refrigerator for up to 4 weeks, or in the freezer for up to 2 months.

Herb Jelly

Rosemary or sage jelly paired with cheese biscuits or roasted chicken is a winner-winner-winner! Also great with lamb: just add garlic to the jelly and baste the meat before grilling or roasting.

Yield 3 (½ pint) jars

6 tablespoons finely chopped herbs
1¼ cups boiling water
¼ cup white wine vinegar
3 cups sugar

Drops food coloring (see below)
1 pouch liquid pectin

Put herbs in boiling water and steep for 15 minutes.

Transfer 1 cup of the herb liquid with herbs to another saucepan for making the jelly.*

Stir in vinegar and sugar, and bring to a boil.

Add food coloring and pectin, and bring to boil for 1 minute, stirring constantly.

Remove saucepan from heat. Skim mixture and pour into sterilized jars. Cover tightly.

Refrigerate when cool; keeps in refrigerator for up to 2 weeks.

*Don't strain out the herbs. You want to see them in the final product.

Rosemary Jelly: 4 tablespoons chopped rosemary and yellow food coloring.

Sage Jelly: 4 tablespoons chopped sage and yellow or green food coloring.

Lemon Balm Jelly: 6 tablespoons chopped lemon balm and green food coloring.

Basic Honey Jelly

Pancakes. Sunday morning. Your favorite newspaper. Why wait?

Yield ½ pint

1 cup honey
¼ cup water
2 tablespoons liquid pectin

Heat honey and water to boiling, stirring constantly.

Add liquid pectin and return to a boil. Stir vigorously for 1 minute before removing from heat.

Pour into sterilized jar. Cool completely before refrigerating. Will keep for 3 weeks.

Red Currant Jelly

Mix with cream cheese and serve with fancy schmancy crackers.

Yield 5 (½ pint) jars

4 pounds red currants
1 cup water
6–7 cups sugar*
1 package powdered pectin

Crush the currants and place in a heavy saucepan. Add the water.

Bring to a boil, then simmer for 10 minutes, stirring frequently.

Remove from heat and strain into a bowl through a cheesecloth-lined sieve.

Reserve 5 cups of the juice.

Return to the saucepan, add the sugar, and bring to a boil on high heat.

Add the pectin immediately upon reaching the boiling point. Stir for ½ minute.

Skim foam from the top and pour jelly into sterilized jars.

Let cool before refrigerating.

Keeps for 3–4 weeks in the refrigerator.

*Sugar amount depends on whether you prefer a more tart or sweet taste.

Guava Jelly

As a toddler, my son's favorite food was guava with *anything*. Today, as a young adult, he eats Guava Jelly straight out of the jar. I say, "Son, how about putting that on a biscuit?" and he mumbles with his mouth full, "No, Mama, it's perfect all alone." For everyone else, I say this is delicious to the nth degree, especially on banana bread, nut breads, and drizzled over fresh fruits.

Yield 2–3 (½ pint) jars

1 can (12-ounce) Hawaii's Own Guava Raspberry* frozen juice, undiluted
2 cups sugar
Juice of 1 small lime
1 package powdered pectin

In a medium saucepan, combine juice with sugar. Cook over medium heat until the sugar dissolves, then simmer until it reaches a syrupy consistency, about 5 minutes.

Add lime juice to the mixture and bring to a boil for an additional 1 minute.

Stir in the pectin and bring back to a boil for 1 minute more, stirring vigorously.

Pour into prepared jars and cover tightly. Cool before refrigerating.

Keeps for 2 weeks in the refrigerator.

*Other brands of frozen or canned guava juice can be substituted.

Ginger Jelly

One of my personal faves. A delicious combination of sweet with a subtle *zip* across your palate. Spread generously on toast, bagels, or even chocolate pound cake! "But I don't like ginger," you protest. Try this. You'll be converted.

Yield 1 pint

1 large apple
¾ cup peeled and freshly chopped gingerroot
¾ cup sugar
1 cup water
1 pouch liquid pectin

Peel and core the apple, then chop it finely.

Combine all ingredients, except pectin, and cook over medium heat until mixture begins to thicken, about 25 minutes.

Add the pectin and bring to a boil for 1 minute, stirring constantly.

Pour in sterilized jars and cover tightly. Refrigerate.

Will keep 3–4 weeks in the refrigerator.

Christmas Jelly

A quick jelly to prepare before Christmas Eve and dot onto thumbprint cookies for Santa. You and the other elves get the leftovers.

Yield 1 pint

1 teaspoon unflavored gelatin

1 2/3 cups unsweetened
   apple juice, divided

2 teaspoons lemon juice

3–4 drops red food coloring

2 teaspoons cinnamon

1/2 teaspoon cloves

1/8 tablespoon allspice

5 tablespoons plus
   1 teaspoon sugar

Bloom, or soften, the gelatin in 1/4 cup apple juice.

Combine remaining apple juice, lemon juice, and food coloring in a saucepan. Boil approximately 7–8 minutes to reduce by one-third. Remove from heat.

Stir spices into the sugar. Stir sugar mixture into hot jelly until sugar dissolves.

Add gelatin and stir thoroughly.

Pour into sterilized jars. Cover tightly.

Store in refrigerator for up to 3 weeks.

Cinnamon Jelly

The red candies make it pretty and remind you of Christmas. Children particularly love this poured over pancakes.

Yield 2 (½ pint) jars

4 cups apple cider
1 pouch liquid pectin
½ cup red cinnamon candies
4½ cups sugar

Pour the apple cider into a 6–8 quart saucepan and add pectin. Stir together.

Add the candies and stir. Cook on high heat until the mixture reaches a full rolling boil.

Add the sugar, bring back to a boil and continue for 1 minute, stirring constantly.

Remove from heat and skim the foam from the top.

Pour into sterilized jars and cover tightly. Cool completely before refrigerating.

Keeps in refrigerator for up to 4 weeks.

Champagne Jelly

Beautiful—like a pale, platinum jewel. Anything you spread it on becomes extraordinary. Everyone who tries it feels that you consider them special.

Yield 4 (½ pint) jars

1 package powdered pectin	3 cups champagne or dry white wine
¾ cup water	4 cups sugar

Thoroughly mix pectin and water in a large saucepan. Bring to a boil and continue boiling for 1 minute, stirring constantly.

Reduce heat to medium and immediately add the champagne and sugar. Keep mixture just below boiling and stir until sugar dissolves, about 5 minutes.

Remove from heat and skim off the foam.

Pour quickly into sterilized jars and cover tightly.

Let cool, then refrigerate.

Keeps in refrigerator for 3–4 weeks.

Faux Champagne Jelly

Prepare the same as for Champagne Jelly, except use a nonalcoholic faux champagne such as *Martinelli's* or your grocery store house brand.

Wine Jelly

Merlot makes this memorable. Rich body, a hint of sweetness, and very elegant. Paired with bite-sized biscuits or mini muffins, elegant crackers, cheeses, fruits, whatever your imagination dreams, this will deliver big at a party.

Yield 1 pint

2 cups robust red wine (merlot or burgundy)
3 cups sugar
1 pouch liquid pectin

Combine wine and sugar in a saucepan and cook on medium-high heat at a bubbly (not rolling) boil for 10 minutes, until sugar dissolves and wine is very hot, stirring occasionally.

Skim foam off top.

Remove from heat and stir pectin into the liquid.

Return briefly to heat until set (about 5–7 minutes), then pour into jelly jars and cover tightly. Refrigerate.

Can be refrigerated for up to 4 weeks.

Orange Sauterne Jelly

This makes a delicious glaze for seafood. Also excellent as a warm sauce for ice cream or fresh berries.

Yield 4 (½ pint) jars

3½ cups fresh orange juice, strained
3 cups sugar, divided
1½ cups sauterne
   (or other good white wine)

1 teaspoon fresh lemon juice
1 package powdered pectin
6 sprigs fresh tarragon *(optional)*

Place orange juice, 2¼ cups sugar, wine, and lemon juice in a heavy saucepan. Stir while cooking on medium-high heat until the sugar dissolves, about 5 minutes.

Mix together ¾ cup sugar and the pectin. Add to the wine mixture.

Cook over high heat, stirring constantly. Boil for 1 minute.

Remove from heat and skim foam from the top.

Add the sprigs of fresh tarragon just before pouring jam into jars.

Place in sterilized jars and cover tightly.

Keeps in the refrigerator for up to 6 weeks.

Mimosa Jelly

This takes your brunch or dinner party to another level. Serve it only when you're out to impress! Great on English muffins, poppy seed bread, or orange muffins; delish drizzled over spongecake or angel food cake.

Yield 4 (1 cup) jars

1½ cups champagne*
1½ cups orange juice
2 small oranges

3 cups sugar
1 pouch liquid pectin

Combine the champagne and orange juice in a heavy saucepan.

Peel oranges and remove the white pith. Chop oranges, then add to saucepan.

Measure the sugar precisely and add it to the liquid.

Bring to a rolling boil and stir constantly until mixture becomes syrupy, about 6–7 minutes.

Add the pectin and stir constantly for 1 minute.

Skim the foam from the top and remove from heat.

Pour into sterilized jars and cover tightly. Allow to cool before refrigerating.

Keeps up to 3 weeks in the refrigerator, but it won't last that long!

*Can substitute sparkling apple cider.

INDEX

METRIC CONVERSION CHART

VOLUME MEASUREMENTS		WEIGHT MEASUREMENTS		TEMPERATURE CONVERSION	
U.S.	Metric	U.S.	Metric	Fahrenheit	Celsius
1 teaspoon	5 ml	1/2 ounce	15 g	250	120
1 tablespoon	15 ml	1 ounce	30 g	300	150
1/4 cup	60 ml	3 ounces	90 g	325	160
1/3 cup	75 ml	4 ounces	115 g	350	180
1/2 cup	125 ml	8 ounces	225 g	375	190
2/3 cup	150 ml	12 ounces	350 g	400	200
3/4 cup	175 ml	1 pound	450 g	425	220
1 cup	250 ml	2 1/4 pounds	1 kg	450	230